Broke

Joan Colby

FUTURECYCLE PRESS

www.futurecycle.org

Published by FutureCycle Press
Lexington, Kentucky, USA

ISBN 978-1-938853-90-6

To my grandsons
Devin and Liam Kelly, Daniel and Jeffrey Pape,
and Parker Colby

Contents

First the toy,
then the heart.
A seiche of tears.
Old foundations erode
breakwaters of despair.

Bad breaks.
Denied promotion.
Flooded basements where
stored treasures float
and rot, sodden with years
of failed transcriptions.

When a wave breaks,
it's opportune. The surfer rises,
achieves a balance the inner ear
controls with coils and sea chants.

Here, where the star-froth
concludes the task of collapse,
broken shells await the
stoopers.

Fault line where the crack was mended
devalues the vase on Antique
Roadshow. If only some careless
ancestor (or maybe you, yourself)
had not allowed that slip of hand:
irremediable loss. Then blame,
that holy glue, suggests
a good-as-new deception.
You blink the barely visible
damage. White line where the scrutiny
of an expert in breakage
will not be denied. Incurable
as heartache. This heirloom. This
imperfection. How the worth
of anything involves condition.

Just past the wire, the fabled filly
undefeated, until now, by her own fragility.
The cannon bone cracks audibly
and, three-legged, she tries to keep
momentum as the jockey vaults off,
seizing the cheek-strap of the bridle.
The crowd, bewildered, hushes.
A cloth shield blocks what's going to happen.
She's down struggling while the jockey
holds her frantic head, eye rolling
as the trainer leaps the rail.
The audience sees nothing.
In solemn tones, the announcer says
the vets are evaluating her prospects
though like everyone beyond that veil
he knows.They don't shoot horses
anymore. A needle full of sleep.
She goes down in the record books.
Best three-year-old of her generation.
Buried, maybe, in the infield,
heart and hooves at least.
Not like a cheap claimer
dragged off to the boneyard.

The sun broke through the clouds
and day was conceivable,
magenta hemmed in gold.
A seabird silhouetted,
its squawk birthing hungers,
barges trawling a harbor's garbage.
See the prows break the water
into splinters of light—
such extraordinary breakage
and waste. So nothing wasted is lost,
but it feeds a desperate blood-hunger
that each day awaits
a stained horizon.

The body sheds
discursive plaints to embrace
chaos. The backward flip
into the text of revolution.
Spin and twirl, out of sync
with measured steps.
The flailing limbs induce
discord and joy,
spell what the body can dispose:
clause, comma, semicolon.
The crooked delight
of question mark,
exclamation point.

Glass eye to the outer world
exists to be broken. Anything thrown—
a child's ball, an enemy's stone,
the rock a spinning tire expels—
can do the job. Fangs of dismay
score the room. A gunshot draws
a perfect hole. Once, taxes limited
installation. The chilly
dark abodes of the poor
where there was nothing
to be broken. Live here
without dodge or hope.

He made and lost fortunes,
cornered the silver market,
went bust in the depression
of the 1880s. Married well,
financed inventions, a mansion
on the Hudson. Newport summer cottage,
lodge in the Adirondacks.

A plutocrat's tale.
The hackneyed Great American Novel,
written, critiqued, abandoned.
A story of manifest destiny,
westward expansion, blood
and vainglory that he believed
like any immigrant
dazzled with ambition.
Streets of gold molten as manure.
He dies broke or
rich and friendless,
the moral lesson
such epics demand.

A biography invented.
How she broke into the movies, discovered
at the seashore or soda fountain
innocently tanning or sipping a malt.
Small town sweetheart tap-dancing
into America's heartland. Years later,
the *ingénue* roles no longer suit—
weary formulas of older sister
or discarded wife fail to pay off
the sluggard who squanders her savings or
the Beverly Hills bungalow. She releases a
tell-all tale of seduction, pills, and booze
to finance the next inexorable breakdown.

Breakouts require revolvers sculpted
of Ivory soap or knotted sheets
strung seven stories to a courtyard
or a laundry cart beneath soiled
linens, a helicopter commandeered
by an ex-wife or the sheer nerve
to seize a guard's gunbelt as you rise
for the verdict. Once, bad men
would storm the jail to free you,
a fast horse saddled, or the lynch mob would
release you to the rope.

Gasping in the sparse bed of age,
you simply stretch forth your hand
and—like that—you're out.

The mahogany china cabinet,
its pediment broken.
Its burden of ruby goblets.
Gold-scalloped dishes from a lost century.
An alphabet mug from which
five generations of children
gulped sweet milk.

Remembering how it stood
in her proper dining room
before age broke her
into a comma curled in a cot.

When we were asked to choose,
this is what we took.

Heroic couplets are now passé
as a broken shield. The poets who met
Ares' red-handed and ennobled
lyric with a lion's victorious roar
are now scorned as old-fashioned,
their Tennysonian lack of irony
embarrassing to an era content to grapple
with dementia, colon cancer, a crippled heart.
The sort of agonies we're all in for.

The New Madrid fault
underlies the heartland.
A century or more since it broke
the Mississippi's commerce,
reversing the flow
the way a promise can be forsaken.
Since then, while the West Coast
renounced pacifism again and again—
bridges and buildings collapsing
to their knees like penitent women
whose men, away at war, wrote the
just-in-case letters—since then
the Missouri farmers wait
just in case the ancient break
should engage the seizures
that refute the common sense
of a state of mind whose motto is
Show Me.

A break, that pause where you
catch your breath for the allotted 15 minutes
contracted by labor. Unlike long-ago
toilers, you can take a rest
and live a decade longer.
Then it's all breakage, going broke
with boredom on the proverbial
porch, your accumulation of lost
time cluttering your mind with
crumbs of remembrance—
as if reverie could compensate.

She vacates the car.
Party over, alone after midnight
on a forsaken road
she doesn't recognize.

She just remembers
how he took off with some ex-girlfriend
as she chugged jello shots and smoked
enough dope to silk her mood.

In the rain, she staggers
to the one farmhouse
visible in arc-light,
an ark of safety, a porch
with a swing and hanging baskets
of dark foliage.

She bangs on the screen door
until a heavy shape fills the doorframe,
opening her mouth on words
as he levels the shotgun and fires,
full in her face, then sees

it's just a girl collapsing like the
drenched flowers, his mind whirling
with stories of home invasions, how
you must protect your property,
a constitutional right—
like the gun.

The night blurs with rain.
What was it she yelled
in that singular instant. Broke down.
Something broke.

Omen of mortality:
broken hip. Maybe a fall
or simply turning in the bed.
Bones blossoming with the
chrysanthemums of fracture.

The rotting plantation of advanced age.
All the servants absconding
with the silver. Femur failing to knit.
Broken as a window
that once shone with resolve.

Shindig of landscape.
The Missouri Breaks
where the river jolts topography
into a sensuous rebuttal of
the declarative sentence. A disharmony
of acoustics. Bar songs. The karaoke of
willful amateurs. Here the badlands
erect haunted castles of shadow.
At sunset, the spectrum of ghosts
breaks into coloratura arias.
Thunderheads to the west
march with bassoons and cymbals.
A flagellated geography
to break your heart.

Laced with scorn
to refute any suggestion of
repair, mending the fractured
dish of estrangement or merely
to demean well-meant
words. Hard-mouthed in the chair
of judgment, a comment that means
to be mean—
Give me a break.

Immobilizer. Hip to ankle
contraption to secure the
wired patella. Straight-legged,
unbending. Heavy.
Gravity hauls its straps
that require perpetual
tightening—six to eight weeks
in this. Caution: must be worn
at all times without surcease.
An element like the Iron Maiden
entrapping bone and flesh. Devil
Cage for the broken. See how one clumps,
fixated, bearing the weight. To heal,
this is required. Like penance, the counted
paces are all recorded.

Rembrandt's dark oils fevered with afterglow
foreshadowing bankruptcy and abandonment.
Modigliani's long-necked ladies of
dissolute absinthe.
Poe inebriated with casks,
black cats and ravens.
Keats dying too young on the bitter
Spanish Steps, his name "writ in water."
El Greco's astigmatic elongations scorned.
Toulouse-Lautrec infected by the gaudy
whores he worshipped.
O. Henry's brief spendthrift ironies.
Gauguin's brown women of jungle dreams
misunderstood, ignored.
Vermeer's pearl earring of hopeless debt.
Wilde's sad coda of cheap hotels.
Melville's obituary "long-forgotten."
Stephen Foster's Swanee River flooding
into Bellevue; in his pocket, 38 cents and a note,
"dear friends and gentle hearts."
Van Gogh, destitute in a starry night of suicide:
"The sadness will last forever."

First strike of the clapper
cracked the rim. Omen of the split
defined by Jefferson and Adams
widening into a civil war.
Philosophical conflict to underscore
the dream of union. Blame
placed on the London foundry,
substituting tin for pure copper.
A divisive economy. Brittle alloy
of the rapscallions. Or damaged in transit.
The fault of an overzealous striker.
Always enough to mask the truth
with a fallible mixture of
heated metals—the great bell of
Liberty damaged at the outset.

To break. To tame. To compel
obedience. Throwing rig.
Sacking. Or just bucking out
until lathered into submission.
Dead broke. Bomb-proof. Dull-eyed.

Or whisper. The ancient technique
of haze. How the horse finds its stance
in the herd. See how it follows,
head nodding, soft-eyed.

O, love, there is always another way.

Blood scours the brow
as stitches are set. Now
a kind of snowing with darts
like ravens flying. Or smoke.
A wave of sunflower breaks
against the wall that shades
into an undersea grotto green. The
vitreous gel has shifted; words blur.
The world is silly with disjunctions.
The spectrum won't behave,
dancing into wrongness like
a willful child. Blink and squint
until the text congeals
into words that can be trusted.

Either a mini-twister or a micro-burst.
A line of big trees that led
to the woodlot broken, some torn
up by the roots, so the grotesque faceprints
stare at us with disregard. Others sheared
or split down the middle as if the sword
of an archangel descended. The ragged souls
of withering leaves already purgatorial.
The woods themselves untouched as if
a community of green prayer could prevail.
O, twisted box elder, cherry, ash,
the roar as you fell into the wind's
intercession. We chainsaw all that is
left of prominence into neat
chunks to fit the wood stove.
Next winter, fire will startle you
into a voice we remember.

She removes the cast for tryouts,
arguing "I pitched the championship
game with this hand." Then undiagnosed
but peculiarly swollen; the orthopedist warns of
deformity, but she won't be
dissuaded. Voted Most Valuable Player.
Her parents dismayed, but fifteen is an age
of obstinacy and obsession. She makes
Junior Varsity again and smiles,
wrapping the elastic bandage around
the support in a perfect figure-eight pattern.

Mouth ajar in the mid-stage of
Huntington's, she peers for speech.
The therapist holding up cards
that another stricken woman
attempts to pronounce, rebooting
the landscape of the brain.
A man climbs a little staircase
to nowhere, his leg in a brace,
and a girl pedals the recumbent bike
on a thruway to recovery. Black shirts
and stretch pants single out the helpers
who joke of last weekend's marathon,
aching glutes and weary abs.
The man with a broken hip groans,
lying on a mat, hefting his purple leg
in the prescribed exercise. Others punch pegs
into holes for dexterity or fold clothes
and make the bed in the sector designed
as a typical home. Home: the goal.
Snorting and clumping in the
skeletal frames of walkers.
One old woman says "Leave me alone."
But they won't. They won't.

The easy way is crossing lawns despite
forbidding signs. Footprints sink into
the dew-soaked grass, despoiling
permanence. It's like cheating
on a math test, the cribbed
equations inked on palms, or
texting your best friend's lover
to set up an assignation
at a beachfront B&B off-
season. What's easy is almost
always wrong. It's like the way you
break the hardback's spine
to read in bed in comfort
despite the pages
loosened or lost.

Patella wired in a figure eight
within a square. Looks good, says the
surgeon. In 12 weeks, it should be healed.
The therapist smiles, says a year
before you'll flex normally.
It's just at 45 degrees now.
Take care to wear the hated brace
or it could buckle. Beware
of missteps, the lack of patience
that toppled you into the chrome
sanctuary of machines: treadmill,
spinning bike, squat slides,
ankle weights, leg lifts, sheer
frustrating repetitions. The X ray shows
a figure eight within a square—
the symbol for extinction.

Acknowledgments

Some of these poems first appeared in *Dead Snakes,
First Literary Review-East, Pyrokinection, The Linnets Wing,*
and *Verse-Virtual.*

*Cover artwork, "The Boneyard" by Pete Linforth;
extinction symbol by A. Zeteki (extinctionsymbol.info);
cover and interior book design by Diane Kistner;
Tahoma text and Arial Black titling*

About FutureCycle Press

FutureCycle Press is dedicated to publishing lasting English-language poetry books, chapbooks, and anthologies in both print-on-demand and ebook formats. Founded in 2007 by long-time independent editor/publishers and partners Diane Kistner and Robert S. King, the press incorporated as a non-profit in 2012. A number of our editors are distinguished poets and writers in their own right, and we have been actively involved in the small press movement going back to the early seventies.

The FutureCycle Poetry Book Prize and honorarium is awarded annually for the best full-length volume of poetry we publish in a calendar year. Introduced in 2013, our Good Works projects are anthologies devoted to issues of universal significance, with all proceeds donated to a related worthy cause. Our Selected Poems series highlights contemporary poets with a substantial body of work to their credit; with this series we strive to resurrect work that has had limited distribution and is now out of print.

We are dedicated to giving all of the authors we publish the care their work deserves, making our catalog of titles the most diverse and distinguished it can be, and paying forward any earnings to fund more great books.

We've learned a few things about independent publishing over the years. We've also evolved a unique, resilient publishing model that allows us to focus mainly on vetting and preserving for posterity the most books of exceptional quality without becoming overwhelmed with bookkeeping and mailing, fundraising activities, or taxing editorial and production "bubbles." To find out more about what we are doing, come see us at www.futurecycle.org.

www.ingramcontent.com/pod-product-compliance
Lightning Source LLC
Chambersburg PA
CBHW060046050426
42448CB00012B/3130